THE GAME OF

SPHAIRISTIKÈ.

THE GAME OF
SPHAIRISTIKE,

DEDICATED TO THE

Party assembled at Nantclwyd

IN DECEMBER, 1873.

BY

Walter Wingfield

HARRISON AND SONS 59, PALL MALL.

ENTERED AT STATIONERS' HALL.]

BY HER MAJESTY'S ROYAL

LETTERS  PATENT.

FRENCH & CO.,

46, CHURTON STREET,

LONDON, S.W.

SPHAIRISTIKÈ.

L'histoire nous l'apprend : de tous les jeux d'adresse
La paume est le plus beau qu'ait inventé la Grèce ;
Périclès et Socrate, Aristide et Zénon
Y jouaient, de leur temps, au pied du Parthénon.
Chacun se délassait ainsi d'être grand homme.
Bientôt, avec les arts, ce jeu passa dans Rome,
Et l'on sait que Caton, le plus grand des Romains,
A ce noble plaisir prêtait ses nobles mains.
César, même César, après une sortie,
Allait au champ de Mars pour faire sa partie.

AUGUSTE ROUSSEL.

THE GAME OF TENNIS may be traced back to the days of the ancient Greeks, under the name of σφαιριστικὴ, and the Athenians showed the estimation in which they held the game by according the rights of citizenship, and in erecting statues to Ariston of Carystius, a player who excelled at this exercise. It appears, from

A

Pliny, that both the Greeks and Romans had Spæristeria, or places appropriated to games of ball. Homer relates, in the VIth Ode of the Odyssey, how white-armed Nausicaa, playing at the game with her handmaidens, hit the ball into the river, and how, in the search for it, they discovered Ulysses. Nausicaa appears to have stood her ground, while the fair-haired damsels very properly fled from the naked shipwrecked warrior.

It was subsequently played by the Romans under the name of " PILA." Horace, in the Vth Satire, in which he describes his journey from Rome to Brundusium, tells how, at one of their halts, Mæcenas, the energetic and fashionable man of the day, goes to play at Tennis while he and Virgil go to sleep. If Horace had played at Tennis, he would not have been so fat. It was the fashionable pastime of the nobles of France, during the reign of Charles V.;

Louis X., François I., Henry IV., Le Duc de Nemours, and Louis XIV. were all enthusiasts at the game. Louis X. was found dead in a grotto, where he had imprudently retired to cool himself after a hard rubber.

It is probable that the game originally did not differ much from " Fives." It is stated that until the 15th century the ball was struck with the bare hand, whence, according to Pasquier, the French appellation of " Paume." Afterwards the hand was protected by a stout glove, still occasionally used by the Basques, and a Racket was substituted about the commencement of the 16th century, and it was in vogue in England as early as Henry III., and is described by Gregory as " one of the most ancient games in Christendom." Henry V., Henry VII., Henry VIII., and Charles II. were all Tennis players, and it has only now died out, owing to the difficulties of the game, and the expense of erecting Courts. All these difficulties have been now surmounted by the inventor of " Sphairistikè," which has all the interest of " Tennis," and has the advantage that it may be played in the open air in any weather by people of any age and of both sexes. In a hard frost the nets may be erected on the ice, and the players being equipped with skates, the game assumes a new feature, and gives an opening for the exhibition of much grace and science.

Croquet, which of late years has monopolized the attention of the public, lacks the healthy and manly excitement of " Sphairistikè," whilst Badminton is simply Battledore and Shuttlecock over a string, and not suitable to out of doors.

Moreover, this game has the advantage that, while an adept at Tennis or Racquets would speedily become a really scientific player, the merest tyro can learn it in five minutes sufficiently well for all practical purposes.

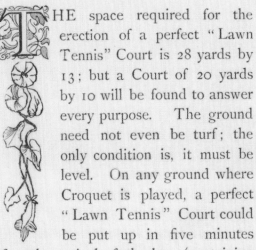

THE space required for the erection of a perfect "Lawn Tennis" Court is 28 yards by 13; but a Court of 20 yards by 10 will be found to answer every purpose. The ground need not even be turf; the only condition is, it must be level. On any ground where Croquet is played, a perfect "Lawn Tennis" Court could be put up in five minutes after the arrival of the box (containing the game); and when once put up, need not be taken down, as the nets are tanned to stand any weather.

Having selected a suitable piece of ground of the size mentioned above, four button-shaped pegs, A, B, C, D,

are placed as in the illustration. The distances at which these pegs are placed from each other to be as nearly as possible the same as given in the illustration.

The distances from A to B and from C to D are 13 yards, and A to C and from B to D are 28 yards, so each Court is 13 yards broad at the base, and 14 yards deep.

The posts E and F will then be placed square across the centre, and the netting stretched betwixt them.

The two wings or side-nettings will then be secured to the posts E and F by the loops and strings attached for the purpose, and the extremities drawn tight in the direction of the pegs A, B, C, D, forming thereby the side walls of the Court, and also the guy* rope to support the posts and centre netting.

Each Court has a line G, H, drawn

---

* Guy ropes are also sent; they will be found round the box. When not playing, ease up your guy ropes.

parallel to the net, and six yards from it; and at right angles to this line is drawn K, L. Ladies may serve from the line G, H, but gentlemen always from the back line of the Court, standing just to the right or left of the centre, with one foot on the line, and serving across, per example, from the line A, K, to Court D.

The boundaries of the Court, and the service creases, may be marked in white, for which purpose a brush will accompany the box, and a mixture of chalk, or lime and water, should be made in a bucket; or they can be made with tape or thatching cord, and pegged down with hair pins, or marked out with a mowing machine.

The side nets are most essential to the marking out of the Courts, and add much to the elegance of the appearance of the game; they are a guide to the eye, and the Courts would not be formed without them.

B

RULES.

I.

THIS game can be played by two or four players.

II.

The sides having been made, and the one to go in having been determined on, as in Racquets, they select their Court, and the first player, standing in the service line, serves, which he does by throwing up the ball with his left hand into the air, and while falling striking it with his bat and sending it over the net between E and F, first into one Court, and then into the other. The out-side stand, one

in the right and the other in the left
Court of the other side; if they fail to
return the ball served to them during
its first bound, or by a "volley," that
is, hitting it before it has touched the
ground, the in-side score an ace; but if
they do return it, the ball is hit back-
wards and forwards over the net till one
side fails to do so, or hits it out of
Court.

III.

The game consists of 15 aces, and
the out-side have the option of setting
it, if they should happen to be 13 or 14
all, to either 3 or 5.

IV.

The outer side can never score an
ace, he can merely put his opponent's
hand out; the score can only be made
by the side that is in.

V.

With four players, the side that goes in has only one hand the first round, afterwards each player has an innings; and when all the players on the side are out, the out-side become the in-side; but they retain the same Courts till the termination of the game. At the conclusion of each game the sides change Courts.

VI.

If the server does not hit the ball over the net between E and F, or sends it out of Court, or fails twice running to serve it into the proper Court, his hand is out.

VII.

If the server sends the ball into the wrong Court, the player in that Court may take it; but he cannot enter his partner's Court and take one that pitches there.

VIII.

A ball that hits the top of the net and goes over, is playable, except in serving, when it must be sent clear over. A ball that alights on the outer lines of the Court is a Let, but a Let is playable at the option of the striker.

IX.

No ball is playable if it does not pass between the posts E and F, even if it may be hit from one Court into a Court on the other side.

X.

A ball that is hit at, even if it is not touched by the bat, or if it afterwards pitches out of Court, is considered as taken.

XI.

A ball may not be hit twice, or taken, if it has previously come in contact with either player.

XII.

The net should be kept tight between the posts E and F, and should be 4 feet 4 inches high in the centre; and players serving from the back crease being 14 yards from the net, may hit the ball overhand, and cut it in any way they can; the service should be from near the centre, as the side nets and lines are all drawn with that idea. In Racquets, though you serve from the side, you serve against a wall, and it is returned into the Court from the centre of the wall.

No Rule can be laid down about placing the players in the Court, as it all depends on the hitting and style of play of the adversaries, whether one player takes the In Court from between the net and the line (G H) and the other the remainder; or, whether one takes the left and the other the right of the Court.

Handicaps.

BETWEEN uneven players the best way of giving points is to make the better player hit every ball over the line G H throughout the game; this is about equivalent to 4 points. If this is not enough, the good player must return each ball into one Court only, which is equivalent to giving 10 points. These Handicaps are better than giving points or extra innings, particularly in the case of ladies, as the ball is returned straight to them, and saves them much running about; besides, the better player will continue to have an object in the game, as it will take all his skill to return the ball into the required space.

Opinions of the Press.

Court Journal.

"SPHAIRISTIKÈ, or Lawn Tennis, the new rival to croquet, has been most favourably reviewed by all the public journals. They declare that it is a clever adaptation of Tennis; that it will become a national pastime; that no English home, no public grounds, no barrack square, should be without it! We certainly wish it well, as it is felt that there is a sad want of a new game—croquet being declared by some too scientific, by others to be an insipid game; whilst the other candidate for public favour, 'Badminton,' cannot be played out of doors except in the stillest weather. Lawn Tennis has been tested at several country houses, and has been found a great success. The game is in a box not larger than a double gun-case, and contains a portable Tennis-court, four bats, and a supply of balls. The court can be erected on any level lawn, and is most ornamental in appearance. What more acceptable present for the Easter holidays can be given than a box of Lawn Tennis?"

Army and Navy Gazette.

"A new game has just been patented by Major WINGFIELD, late 1st Dragoon Guards, which, if we mistake not, will become a national pastime. 'Lawn Tennis'—for that is the

C

name under which the game makes its appearance—is a clever adaptation of Tennis to the exigencies of an ordinary lawn or level piece of ground, the space required for a perfect Lawn Tennis-court being merely 20 yards by 10. It will be seen, therefore, how admirably the game is suited, in this respect, to the barrack yard and parade ground. We would advocate its adoption in every barrack square throughout the Kingdom, not merely because of its intrinsic merits as a game, but because, also, we believe it would be found to relieve the monotony of barrack life, and act as a healthy adjunct to supplement the eternal 'Position Drills,' which are supposed to aid so much in the formation of a rifle shot."

Dundee Advertiser.

" A new game has just been patented which will, if I mistake not, become a national pastime. It is a clever adaptation of Tennis to the exigencies of an ordinary lawn or level ground. It may likewise be played on ice, the players being equipped with skates. It is adapted for people of any age and of both sexes, and as the game has much more healthy and manly excitement than croquet, the chances are it will drive that game out of the field. Tennis has long been known in England as a noble game, but the expense of erecting courts, and the time required to master its intricacies, have restricted it to a fortunate few; but 'Lawn Tennis,' the name now given to this new game, is placed within the reach of the majority of people, and the advent of such a really good game should be hailed as a public boon even at Dundee, where it should not be forgotten that all work and no play is a bad thing. Lawn Tennis has been tested practically at several country houses during the past few months, and has been found a great success. I understand the game will be extensively advertised in the course of the next few days."

Sporting Gazette.

"Whilst speaking of sports, I may pay a passing tribute to the inventor of a new game, which adds another to that too limited list of pastimes in which ladies and gentlemen can join. The name of the new comer, which is to oust croquet from the field and become *the* fashionable lawn game, is 'Sphairistikè!' 'Eh?' Ah! Yes, you may well stare, gentle reader. It is a barbarous name, I grant you, one that would have made 'Quinctilian stare and gasp;' but it simply means Lawn Tennis. Why a less jawbreaking name could not have been found for it is a question which I leave you to settle with the inventor. It is played in the open air by means of a portable court, and I understand it is likely to be an additional feature to the attractions of Polo at Lillie Bridge in the coming season. That will give it the *entrée* into good society, and I have no doubt that before another twelvemonth has passed, it will be a popular pastime in every English home which can boast of a level piece of ground 20 yards by 10. Let croquet look to its laurels. I confess myself to a strong liking for croquet; but it has become too scientific now to please ordinary loungers of both sexes, who only care for something which will serve *pour passer le temps*, and enable them to enjoy fresh air and flirtation in agreeable combination. You are tired of croquet, come with me and let us try our hands at 'Sph-Sph-Sphair—.' No!—I don't mind playing it, but I will *not* undergo the torture of pronouncing it; that is too much to expect. I content myself with the last syllables, 'Stikè.' Ladies and gentlemen, take my advice, and give 'Stikè' a trial, *vice* croquet, temporarily deposed."

The Globe.

"A REVIVAL OF TENNIS.

"It will hardly be denied that the time is fully come for the inauguration of a new out-door game. By the term 'game,' we mean something very distinct from a 'sport,' of which genus we have just now enough—perhaps to spare; something, that is, eminently social, sociable, and comfortable, as opposed to the breathless, violent, and more or less painful exercises which constitute modern athletics. Of such milder diversions, more truly called amusements, there has been for two or three years a terrible dearth. The ancestral bowling green, even where it has survived, is voted much too slow; archery involves too large a space, too elaborate paraphernalia, and, last but not least, too much hard work to be ever again widely popular; and croquet, now that its first frantic burst of success has died away, is weighed in the balance and found, at least in a social point of view, a complete failure. The owners of country houses, the givers of *fêtes champêtres,* and, in fine, all those benevolent persons who spasmodically attempt to bring together into some sort of harmony and amity the rugged, ungenial members of country society, are consequently at their wits' end for some attraction wherewith to fill their lawns in the summer time. All these people—and may their numbers never grow less— will heartily thank Major WINGFIELD for a brave attempt he is now making to fill up the gap at present so apparent. He has invented and patented a new out-door game, which, like all happy inventions, appears the simplest and most obvious thing possible now that it is once fairly in the field. The game is nothing but an adaptation of the old game of Tennis to a common open lawn, whereupon, as it now appears, an arrangement of the most simple kind enables it to be played with immense success. Of course every new invention must in these days have an unintelligible, or at least, almost unintelligible name, or nobody would believe in it. Accordingly, Major WINGFIELD has christened his game 'Sphairistikè,' and, by way of extra attraction, writes the appalling Greek word in Greek characters—doubtless on the now well-recognised trade principle of *omne ignotum pro magnifico.* For the benefit of those who have not cultivated the Attic muse, it may be explained that the word is apparently intended to be a translation of 'Tennis,' although it is not really so, but signifies 'the art of playing at Tennis.' However, the inaccuracy is extremely pardonable, since it adds a length, and therefore a dignity, to the word which would be wanting to a mere 'Sphœresis.' It may be safely assumed that both Greeks and Romans would, if they could be consulted on the subject, freely pardon a much greater liberty on the part of 'the Major,' in consideration of the compliment he pays them in reviving so classical and venerable a game. There is no more curious phrase in the history of games than the decline and fall of Tennis. After having formed part of the 'musical' education of the agile Greeks, and exercised the iron limbs of the Roman warriors, as well as the podgy frame of the poet Horace, it survived the barbarity of the middle ages (for Tennis courts outlived the iconoclastic fury of Vandals and Goths, which was fatal to temples and theatres), and became the fashionable pastime of Western Europe even in the days of tournaments. In England it was played by the 3rd, the 5th, the 7th, and the 8th of our Henries, and was no less popular among the nobles of France. It is only within the present century that its glories have been eclipsed and superseded by the simpler game of racquets, and the growing taste for an easier and less expensive game has consigned it almost to oblivion. There is now in the day of its deepest degradation, some hope that it may resume its sway, shorn indeed of much of its beauty and *finesse,* but free also from the difficulties which have been so fatal.

"The Major's game of 'Lawn Tennis' may be very briefly described. It consists of a pair of upright poles fixed in the ground about ten yards apart, supporting a screen of network stretched between them. From the top of each pole cords are stretched at right angles to the net, and attached to pegs on each side of it. Thus there are two cords and two pegs on each side, and these serve to mark out the boundaries of the two courts occupied by the 'out' and the 'in' players respectively. The game is played by hitting the ball with a racquet bat across the net from side to side alternately, and that player who first fails to hit the ball over into the opposite court loses either an ace or his 'innings,' as the case may be. As soon as one of the sides has won fifteen aces he is, as at racquets, the winner of the game. The players may be, as at Tennis, either one or two a side, and in the latter case the partners each occupy their own side of the court. Among the merits of the game is the fact that it can be played not only on turf, but upon any tolerably flat surface. Barrack yards will be admirable places, and the sea-shore may often be used with great effect. Even a good turnpike road will serve the purpose at a pinch, though the travellers on the Queen's highway would probably have a word to say against this plan. Finally, the whole apparatus, when prettily painted or gilded, has rather an ornamental appearance, and the exercise, whether for gentleman or lady, is as graceful and healthy as croquet is the reverse. The game will, of course, be a rival of 'Badminton' in the ensuing season, but inasmuch as it is both less childish, more novel, and more independent of the influence of wind and weather, it bids fair to eclipse the latter as completely as croquet beat lawn billiards."

Morning Post.

"AN AFTERNOON AT PRINCE'S.

" Meanwhile to the right of the entrance gates two portions of the ground have been set apart for Lawn Tennis. When the modification of battledore and shuttlecock, known by the name of and invented by the players at Badminton, was introduced, it was felt that any form of it which should admit of being played out of doors would be an advantage. Lawn Tennis is the result of this feeling. Tennis proper reached its present stage not a little through the love of exercise not unknown to monastic life; and the Tennis court is probably simply an alteration of the recreation ground of a monastery. But Tennis has never been a game at which ladies could play, while Lawn Tennis, like Badminton, is a game at which ladies can display considerable proficiency. The open-air modification of Badminton gives, therefore, a game in which the delicacy and gentleness of a woman's touch counterbalances the mere strength of a man's arm, and provides an amusement in which both sexes can unrestrainedly share. Of the intricacies of the game, which has already established itself in the gardens of many country houses, and not a few of those London houses in which gardens exist, we may possibly on a future occasion give some account, but at present we content ourselves with observing, that those who are fortunate enough to obtain admission to Prince's have an opportunity of passing a summer afternoon in a way which is enjoyable, healthy, and sociable."

The Daily Telegraph.

"A DAY AT PRINCE'S.

"But even yet the varied pleasures of Prince's are not exhausted. Away, on an extra lawn on the London side of the ground—away from the cricket, away from the mock ice and the real ices—away from the skirts and the bugle-embroidered bodies—from the colour, the costumes, and the fashionable crowd, they are playing 'Sphairistikè' or 'Lawn Tennis,' the new summer game which will make the name of Major WINGFIELD gratefully remembered in many a country house. The monopoly of croquet is at last broken, the sway of the young curate is seriously threatened, the dreary inaction and scientific affectation of the one lawn game are likely to be prevented by a study of the simple invention called 'Lawn Tennis.' We here obtain the excitement of the first of ball games without its intolerable expense; the activity of rackets without the close atmosphere of a court; and the fun of Badminton without depending on a day still enough for the airy shuttlecock. The new game is played on a lawn, with india-rubber balls and an ordinary racket, over a net specially provided, and in a court easily marked out on any smooth turf, or indeed on any level ground. The popularity of Sphairistikè is at once shown by the eagerness with which ladies as well as gentlemen desire to have a turn at it; its rules come as a matter of course to all who as boys have played rackets and fives, and it is learned in a few minutes by any lady watching the game at Prince's. So now, whether the wind blows or whether it is still, in winter or in summer, an active, busy, and amusing exercise has been cleverly provided. There is no damaging the flower beds or hitting among the rose bushes. The most careful gardener and most particular house-owner will not raise an objection when the 'Lawn Tennis' box appears at the country house. The only thing likely to suffer is the hospitable fare at dinner-time, for 'Lawn Tennis' gives rosy cheeks and a huge appetite, and might well be introduced into the innumerable squares and London enclosures now mainly occupied by romping children and literary nursemaids."

Vanity Fair.

LAWN TENNIS.

"The notion of taking a sphere and of playing with it, if not suggested by, appears to be almost as old as the creation of the world. And to this day the most popular and lasting of bodily exercises in every country on the face of this planet are still found to be those which depend upon the manipulation, in some form or other, of a ball. Hockey, Polo, Croquet, Golf, Cricket, Base-Ball, Racquets, Fives, Pallone, Billiards, and any number of other illustrations will at once occur even to those who see no connection between them and the movements of the stars in their courses ; but of all games of ball that which is known as Tennis is by far the best and the most important. Probably of monastic origin, and played originally—as the "penthouse," the "dedans," and the "grille" would all indicate—in the cloisters, it was already a favourite pastime in the Middle Ages. The courtiers of Charles V. of France played it for large sums of money ; our Henry V., if we may trust Shakespeare, was an adept at it ; and Henry VIII. built at Hampton Court what is still the best tennis-court in England. It has come down to us in a pure and unadulterated form, and although, or perhaps because, it takes a lifetime to learn to play and another lifetime to learn to mark the game, it is so varied, so amusing, and gives so much play to intellectual as well as to corporeal activity, that those who possess it cannot but despise all other games whatever.

"Nevertheless, it is not given to many either to possess the physical qualities, or to have at disposal the time required to attain sufficient proficiency in this the queen of all games to find amusement in it. What is required in these hurried times is a game more easily acquired, more readily installed, demanding less exertion, and yet giving sufficient play to judgment, quickness of eye and hand, and acquired skill, to make it worth learning and playing. And above all, what is highly desirable is, that it should so combine all these requirements as to be capable of being played by ladies, or by men, neither very strong, very active, or very ready in the use of their hands and legs. Lawn tennis very fairly unites

D

all these qualities. The machinery required for it, consisting as it does merely of the net and a few racquets and balls, is inexpensive, readily attainable, easily transportable, and capable of being set up on any fairly level open space. The rules are simple and readily learnt, and anybody who can strike a shuttlecock with a battledore may easily acquire sufficient skill to make the game an interesting exercise. How interesting it has already become to many may be judged by going any day to Prince's, and seeing the eagerness with which it is pursued in the most doubtful weather over the most slippery ground, far into the twilight; and there can be no doubt that during the very short time it has existed it has taken quite an important place among English pastimes. It has, indeed, some defects which seem to demand a remedy. The thin India-rubber balls with which it is played vary so considerably in weight and in quality that it is well-nigh impossible to place or to play them with any certainty; and although it would not be advisable to make them as hard as tennis or racquet balls, they might probably be made much harder and denser than they are, and consequently more alike, by simply increasing their thickness and weight. Then the server has rather too great an advantage, since a clean-cut ball passing just over the net into the farthest corner of the opposite court is all but impossible of return. This cannot be fully met by raising the height of the net, since that interferes with the subsequent course of the play; but it might perhaps be dealt with by making an outside service-court some two yards square half a yard outside the centre of each of the two playing-courts. If this service-court were treated as the "dedans" in ordinary tennis, and a stroke into it were allowed to count as an ace, that would give a further interest to the game by increasing the objects to be played for. At present Lawn-Tennis is worth playing ill, which is a great merit in any game, and quite sufficient to render it quickly popular; but if it is to live and take a per-

manent place, it must be worth playing well ; and if by such
modifications as are here indicated, or by any others, this can
be attained, it will become as favourite and as lasting a
pastime as its greater and more immediate original, the open-
air Tennis of the Basque provinces."

The Sporting Gazette.

October 31, 1874.

"I hear from Paris that people are all raving there about
'Sphairistikè.' There was a great run upon the game as
soon as it was discovered that it might be understood and
played without the necessity of pronouncing it. They say
there are only two Frenchmen who can pronounce the name,
and one calls it 'Sphittiky,' and the other "Farsticky."
It has been introduced, too, with success at Colney Hatch,
and after an animated game the other day one of the patients
(an incurable) was heard to ask another, 'Why is the game
of lawn tennis like treacle?' The answer was given with
a demoniac laugh, 'Because it's *very sticky!*' and the
wretched man has been an occupant of the padded cell ever
since. I hear that Major Wingfield has made such a good
thing out of the game, which has become astonishingly
popular all over the world, that he intends bringing out an
indoor game at Christmas with a Latin name, which will
equal, if not surpass, its sesquipedalian Greek brother.
The name, I understand, will not exceed ten syllables, and
may be easily mastered in six lessons. If Major Wingfield
can produce a really good indoor game—and I fancy he will
—then I shall hail him as a benefactor of his species, as the
very Archimedes of amusement."

A full account of the Game, with Illustrations, was also given in "THE FIELD," "LAND AND WATER," and "QUEEN," and the Author has received numerous Testimonials of its excellence.

In testimony of the excellence of this popular Game, the Inventor calls attention to the following List of titled personages who have already bought it.

1st *November*, 1874.

H. R. H. THE PRINCE OF WALES.

H. I. H. THE CROWN PRINCESS OF PRUSSIA.

H. I. H. THE GRAND DUKE CZAREWITCH.

H. R. H. THE DUKE OF EDINBURGH.

H. R. H. PRINCE LEOPOLD.

H. R. H. PRINCESS LOUISE.

H. R. H. PRINCE LOUIS OF HESSE.

PRINCE BATTHYANY.

PRINCE BARIATINSKY.

PRINCE WOLKONSKY.

His Grace the Duke of—

Athole.	Richmond.
Buccleuch.	Somerset.
Devonshire.	St. Albans.
Grafton.	

The Marquis of—

Ailsa.	Hertford.
Aylesbury.	Lansdowne.
Bath.	Londonderry.
Bristol.	Lorne.
Conyngham.	Lothian.
Exeter.	Ripon.
Headfort.	Stafford.

The Marchioness of—

Downshire.	Winchester.

His Excellency The Governor-General of Canada.

The Earl of—

Abingdon.	Dunmore.
Ashburnham.	Durham.
Aylesford.	Erroll.
Bathurst.	Exmouth.
Beauchamp.	Feversham.
Bective.	Galloway.
Bradford.	Glasgow.
Breadalbane.	Granville.
Cadogan.	Haddington.
Camperdown.	Hardwicke.
Carysfort.	Harrington.
Cawdor.	Ilchester.
Clonmell.	Kenmare.
Cottenham.	Kimberley.
Craven.	Langford.
Dalkeith.	Lanesborough.
Darnley.	Leicester.
Dartrey.	Lichfield.

The Earl of—

Listowel.
Lonsdale.
Manvers.
Minto.
Mount-Edgcumbe.
Normanton.
Onslow.

Pembroke.
Salisbury.
Sefton.
Stair.
Wicklow.
Yarborough.

The Countess—

Cowper.
Delaware.
Fitzwilliam.
Grey.
Scarborough.

Shannon.
Spencer.
Sydney.
Waldegrave.
Winchelsea.

Viscount—

Bangor.
Combermere.
Eversley.
Halifax.

Petersham.
Powerscourt.
Stormont.
Walden.

Lord—

Annaly.
Ashburton.
Auckland.
Bolton.
Brabayne.
Burghersh.
Carrington.
E. Cavendish.
A. Churchill.
Churston.
Clinton.

De Ros.
Dunglass.
George Gordon.
Harris.
A. Lennox.
Londesborough.
Norreys.
Ramsay.
Rendlesham.
Rivers.
Ruthven.

Lord—

Walter Scott.	Suffield.
William Seymour.	Wenlock.
Shand.	Willoughby de Broke.
Skelmersdale.	Wharncliffe.

La Baronne Alphonse de Rothschild.
Baron Alfred de Rothschild.
La Marquise de l'Aigle.

Lady—

Edith Ashley.	Mildred Beresford
Bateson (Hon).	Hope.
Blunt.	Hunter.
Buxton.	Huntingfield.
Chesham.	Ingilby (Hon).
De Vesci.	Adeline Larking.
Harriet Dundas.	Frances Legge.
Filmer (Hon.)	Lilford.
Fitzgerald.	Manners.
Fitzhardinge.	Musgrove.
Payne Galloways.	Napier.
Gardner.	Dorothy de Neville.
Gervis.	Alfred Paget.
Grace Gordon.	Penrhyn.
Emily Gore.	Peyton.
W. Graham.	Pilkington.
Hamilton.	Jane Stewart.
Heneage.	Emily Walsh.
Holland.	Willoughby.

Honourable—

Joceline Amherst.	C. Ashley.

Honourable—

F. G. Baring.
G. M. Bennett.
W. Bethell.
Mrs. Birkbeck.
S. Bridgeman (Rev.)
A. Cadogan.
A. Calthorpe.
Mrs. B. Denison.
Cecil Duncombe.
J. C. Dundas.
R. Egerton.
Col. Ellis.
Lieut.-Col. F. Elphin-
stone.
Mrs. Fitzwilliam.
M. F. Hatton.
Lascelles (Rev.)

B. Lawley.
Col. Lindsay.
Mrs. Mure.
R. Neville.
Mrs. Nugent.
Mrs. Parsons.
Ashley Ponsonby.
Mrs. Orde Powlett.
R. Spencer.
Edward Stanhope.
H. Strutt.
Henry Temple.
R. H. Temple.
Mrs. Vernon.
A. Winn.
P. Wyndham.

Right Honourable—

H. B. W. Brand, M.P.,
the Speaker.
W. E. Forster, M.P.

Knatchbull-Hugessen,
M.P.
Mowbray, M.P.

Sir—

Robert Abercromby.
John H. Amory.
G. Armytage.
John Astley.
Thomas Bateson.
Hervy Bruce.
Charles Bunbury.
Gerald Codrington.
Bache Cunard.

Robert Cunliffe.
Henry Dashwood.
Andrew Fairbairn.
Henry Fletcher.
Robert Gerard.
Frederick Graham.
R. Hamilton, Bart.
William Hayter.
E. Hulse.

Sir—

H. Ibbetson.
H. Ingilby.
Col. Clarke Jervoise.
Frederick Johnstone.
Wilfrid Lawson.
E. C. Macnaghten.
W. Marriott.
H. St. John Mildmay.
Charles Mills.
William Milner.
Thomas Moncreiffe.
C. Mordaunt.

George Nugent.
R. Palmer.
Henry B. Peirse.
James Ramsden.
Charles Russell.
Gilbert Scott.
Hamilton Seymcur.
Greville Smith.
Henry Tring.
H. Tufton.
H. Williamson.

37

BY HER MAJESTY'S ROYAL LETTERS PATENT

PRICE LIST

FOR CASH ONLY

	£	s	d
Box of Sphairistike, the game complete as advertised	6	0	0
Extra sized Box with Racquet Press, extra Bats and a supply of balls for several months	10	10	0
The Patent Court complete in box	2	7	6
Racquet Press for 6 Bats	1	0	0
Ditto, Ditto for 4 Bats	0	15	0
Full sized Sphairistike Bats	1	0	0
Ladies Bats		15	0
Balls per dozen	0	5	0
Sphairistike Tape Measures	0	2	6
Tennis Shoes, with India-rubber soles, which will not cut up the turf	0	18	6

BEWARE OF SPURIOUS IMITATIONS

Every Box, Bat and Ball is marked Sphairistike

The bats are expressly made for the game, of the original shape designed by the Inventor, the balls are manufactured in Germany, and made especially of an extra thickness of India rubber, and not procurable anywhere else.

SOLE AGENTS –

MESSRS. FRENCH & CO.

46, CHURTON ST. PIMLICO,

LONDON, S.W.

The following complimentary letter is from a well known Baronet to the Editor of one of the leading London Journals, showing the superiority of Sphairistike over all other games for winter play. It can be played on any level surface:-

Grosvenor Place,

March 11th, 1874.

Dear Sir,

Major Wingfield has asked me to give you my opinion of 'Lawn Tennis', and I can unhesitatingly say it is far and away the best out-of-door game known. It far surpasses croquet or lawn billiards, and I think the best proof I can give you is that a large country house full of men played it all last winter, and their enjoyment of it was so great that the ladies at last joined in the game, and some of them played it remarkably well. The great beauty of the game is, that it can be played on such a very ground, so that no lawn is too small. It is especially suited to winter, as to play it well a great deal of energy and activity is required, and in this particular it will certainly take the place of croquet, as there are none of the long weary pauses between the turns as in croquet. I can highly recommend it as a game, and I am sure you will be doing a good turn to the parties assembled in the country houses if you give it a favourable notice in your well known paper.

I remain, Sir,

Your obedient Servant,